MY CREPE RECIPE BOOK

BY

CARLA HUTSON

Copyright © 2023 by Carla Hutson. All rights reserved.

No part of this book may be reproduced in any form or by any electronic or mechanical means, including information storage and retrieval systems, without written permission from the author, except for the use of brief quotations in a book review.

Table of Contents

Recipe for Crepe 5
Tips For Making Perfect Crepes 6
Shredded Pork, Ham, Chili Paste Crepe 7
Ham Cheddar Pizza Crepe 9
Tuna, Mozzarella, Creamed Corn Crepe 11
Mediterranean Morning Crepes 13
Savory Spinach Feta Crepes 15
Bacon, Egg & Cheese Brunch Crepes 17
Chicken salad Crepes 19
Mushroom & Truffle Oil Delight Crepes 21
Ham, Egg & Cheese Breakfast Crepes 23
Greek Chicken & Feta Savory Crepes 25
Smoked Salmon & Cream Cheese Brunch Crepes 27
Mixed Berry Rainbow Crepes 29
Mango Sticky Rice Crepe 31
Blueberry Bliss Crepes 33
Caramelized Apple Spice Crepes 35
Chocolate Hazelnut Cream Crepes 37
Honey and Raspberry Delight Crepes 39
Sweet Potato Cinnamon Roll Crepes 41
Tiramisu Lover's Crepes 43
Matcha Green Tea Delight Crepes 45
Tropical Island Paradise Crepes 47
Fruit Lovers' Crepes 49
Mochi Brownie Chocolate Crepes 51
Nutella Banana Cereal Crepes 53
Apple Pie Cinnamon Roll Crepes 55

Strawberry Shortcake Delight Crepes 57

Classic French Crepes Suzette (French Crepes with Orange) 59

Honeyed Ricotta, Pistachio Delight And Almond Crepes 61

Peanut Butter Lovers' Crepes 63

Green Tea Crepe With Red Beans 65

Recipe for Crepe

A crepe is a thin pancake made from a batter of flour, eggs, milk, and butter. It originated in France but is now a popular dish worldwide. Crepes can be served with sweet or savory fillings, such as Nutella and fruit, ham and cheese, or spinach and mushroom. The batter is usually spread thinly on a hot flat pan or griddle and cooked quickly on both sides, producing a delicate and slightly crispy texture. Crepes are often served for breakfast, brunch, or dessert and can be made in advance and reheated. They are versatile dishes that can be enjoyed in many different ways.

Recipe for crepe batter:

Ingredients:

- 1 cup all-purpose flour
- 1 1/2 tablespoons sugar
- 1/4 teaspoon salt
- 3 large eggs
- 1 1/4 cups whole milk
- 2 tablespoons unsalted butter, melted and cooled
- 1 teaspoon vanilla extract

Instructions:

1. Whisk together the flour, sugar, and salt in a large mixing bowl.
2. In a separate bowl, beat the eggs until smooth.
3. Gradually add the milk to the eggs, whisking continuously.
4. Add the melted butter and vanilla extract to the egg mixture, and whisk until well combined.
5. Pour the egg mixture into the flour mixture, and whisk until a smooth batter forms.
6. Cover the batter and rest in the refrigerator for at least 30 minutes (or overnight).

How to Serve Crepes

1. Heat a non-stick pan over medium heat.
2. Ladle a small amount of batter onto the pan (about 1/4 cup) and swirl the pan to spread the batter evenly.
3. Cook for 1-2 minutes, until the crepe is lightly browned on the bottom.
4. Flip the crepe and cook for another 30 seconds on the other side.
5. Transfer the crepe to a plate and serve the crepes warm with your desired filling.
6. And repeat with the remaining batter.

Tips For Making Perfect Crepes

1. Use a non-stick pan or a well-seasoned cast iron skillet to prevent the crepes from sticking to the pan.
2. Make sure the pan is hot before adding the batter. You can test the temperature by dropping a small amount of batter onto the pan. If it sizzles and starts to cook immediately, the pan is ready.
3. Use a ladle or measuring cup to pour the batter onto the pan. The amount of batter should be enough to coat the bottom of the pan in a thin layer, but not too much that the crepes become too thick.
4. Use a spatula to loosen the edges of the crepe before flipping it. Gently slide the spatula underneath the crepe to release it from the pan and then use your fingers to flip it over.
5. Cook the crepes on medium heat to ensure they cook evenly and don't burn.
6. Be patient and don't rush the cooking process. Crepes cook quickly, so keep an eye on them and flip them over as soon as the edges start to turn golden brown.

Shredded Pork, Ham, Chili Paste Crepe

Crepes are a delicious and versatile treat that can be served with sweet or savory toppings. With the right ingredients, they can make a great meal that will surely please your taste buds. For an exciting and unique twist on crepes, try out this recipe for Shredded Pork, Ham, and Chili Paste Crepes. This savory delight is packed with flavor from the pork, ham, and chili paste and makes for a delicious meal.

Ingredients:

- ✓ 1 cup all-purpose flour
- ✓ 2 large eggs
- ✓ 1 cup milk
- ✓ 1/4 cup water
- ✓ 1/4 tsp salt
- ✓ 1/4 cup vegetable oil
- ✓ 1/2 cup shredded pork
- ✓ 1/2 cup ham, diced
- ✓ 1 tbsp chili paste
- ✓ 1 green onion, thinly sliced

Instructions:

1. Whisk together flour, eggs, milk, water, salt, and vegetable oil in a mixing bowl until the batter is smooth.
2. Cover the bowl and let the batter rest for at least 30 minutes at room temperature.
3. Mix shredded pork, diced ham, and chili paste in a separate bowl until well combined.
4. Heat a non-stick skillet over medium heat.
5. Pour 1/4 cup of the crepe batter onto the skillet and swirl to evenly spread the batter.
6. Cook the crepe for about 1 minute on one side or until the edges turn golden brown.
7. Flip the crepe over and cook the other side for another 30 seconds.

8. Once all the crepes are cooked, add 1-2 tablespoons of the pork and ham mixture on one-half of the crepe and sprinkle some green onions over it.
9. Fold the other half of the crepe over the filling and gently press down.
10. Serve the crepes warm with extra green onions on top, if desired.
11. Repeat the process with the remaining batter.

Ham Cheddar Pizza Crepe

Pizza is a classic and delicious food with many different ways to enjoy it. One unique way that you can enjoy pizza is in the form of a crepe. Ham Cheddar Pizza Crepes are an easy and tasty dish that can be served for breakfast, lunch, or dinner. This dish combines all of the classic pizza flavors with the lightness of crepes for a delicious meal that your whole family will love.

Ingredients:

- 1 cup all-purpose flour
- 2 large eggs
- 1 cup milk
- 1/4 cup water
- 1/4 tsp salt
- 1/4 cup vegetable oil
- 1/2 cup ham, diced
- 1 cup shredded cheddar cheese
- 1/4 cup pizza sauce
- 1/4 cup sliced black olives (optional)

Instructions:

1. In a mixing bowl, whisk together flour, eggs, milk, water, salt, and vegetable oil until the batter is smooth.
2. Cover the bowl and let the batter rest for at least 30 minutes at room temperature.
3. In a separate bowl, mix together diced ham, shredded cheddar cheese, pizza sauce, and sliced black olives (if using) until well combined.
4. Heat a non-stick skillet over medium heat.
5. Pour 1/4 cup of the crepe batter onto the skillet and swirl to evenly spread the batter.
6. Cook the crepe for about 1 minute on one side or until the edges turn golden brown.
7. Flip the crepe over and cook the other side for another 30 seconds.

8. Once all the crepes are cooked, add 1-2 tablespoons of the ham and cheddar pizza mixture on one-half of the crepe.
9. Fold the other half of the crepe over the filling and gently press down.
10. Place the crepe on a baking sheet and bake in a preheated oven at 350°F for 5-10 minutes, until the cheese is melted and bubbly.
11. Slice the crepes into wedges and serve warm.
12. Repeat the process with the remaining batter.

Tuna, Mozzarella, Creamed Corn Crepe

Ah, crepes! A French classic that has been enjoyed for centuries and is now a popular dish all around the world. Today we'll explore a unique twist on this traditional favorite – Tuna, Mozzarella, and Creamed Corn Crepe. This delectable dish combines savory tuna, creamy cheese, and sweet corn for an unforgettable flavor combination that will tantalize your taste buds.

Ingredients:

- 1 cup all-purpose flour
- 2 large eggs
- 1 cup milk
- 1/4 cup water
- 1/4 tsp salt
- 1/4 cup vegetable oil
- 1 can of tuna, drained and flaked
- 1 cup shredded mozzarella cheese
- 1/4 cup creamed corn
- Salt and pepper to taste
- Tomato sauce and mayonnaise to taste

Instructions:

1. In a mixing bowl, whisk together flour, eggs, milk, water, salt, and vegetable oil until the batter is smooth.
2. Cover the bowl and let the batter rest for at least 30 minutes at room temperature.
3. Heat a non-stick skillet over medium heat.
4. Pour 1/4 cup of the crepe batter onto the skillet and swirl to evenly spread the batter.
5. Cook the crepe for about 1 minute on one side or until the edges turn golden brown.
6. Flip the crepe over and cook the other side for another 30 seconds.
7. Once all the crepes are cooked, add 1-2 tablespoons of the creamed corn, tuna, and mozzarella on one-half of the crepe.

8. Topped with salt, pepper, tomato sauce, and mayonnaise.
9. Fold the other half of the crepe over the filling and gently press down.
10. Place the crepe on a plate and sprinkle some chopped parsley on top.
11. Repeat with the remaining crepes and filling.

Mediterranean Morning Crepes

Nothing quite like the smell of freshly made crepes wafting through your kitchen in the morning. Mediterranean Morning Crepes are a delicious and easy way to start your day with a wholesome breakfast. This recipe will provide an easy-to-follow recipe packed with flavor, texture, and nutrition to satisfy even the pickiest eaters.

Ingredients:

- ✓ 1 cup all-purpose flour
- ✓ 2 large eggs
- ✓ 1 cup milk
- ✓ 1/4 cup water
- ✓ 1/4 tsp salt
- ✓ 1/4 cup vegetable oil
- ✓ 1/4 cup hummus
- ✓ 1/4 cup diced tomatoes
- ✓ 1/4 cup crumbled feta cheese
- ✓ 2 tbsp chopped fresh parsley
- ✓ Salt and pepper to taste

Instructions:

1. In a mixing bowl, whisk together flour, eggs, milk, water, salt, and vegetable oil until the batter is smooth.
2. Cover the bowl and let the batter rest for at least 30 minutes at room temperature.
3. In a separate bowl, mix hummus, diced tomatoes, crumbled feta cheese, and chopped parsley until well combined.
4. Heat a non-stick skillet over medium heat.
5. Pour 1/4 cup of the crepe batter onto the skillet and swirl to evenly spread the batter.
6. Cook the crepe for about 1 minute on one side or until the edges turn golden brown.
7. Flip the crepe over and cook the other side for another 30 seconds.

8. Once all the crepes are cooked, add 1-2 tablespoons of the hummus, tomato, and feta mixture on one-half of the crepe.
9. Fold the other half of the crepe over the filling and gently press down.
10. Place the crepe on a plate and sprinkle some chopped parsley on top.
11. Repeat with the remaining crepes and filling.

Savory Spinach Feta Crepes

Crepes are a delicious and versatile dish that can be enjoyed for breakfast, lunch, or dinner. This Savory Spinach Feta Crepes recipe is perfect for a savory meal that's light yet filling. The crepe batter is simple to make, and the combination of spinach, feta cheese, garlic, and herbs creates an incredible flavor. Best of all, these crepes are easy to customize so that you can customize them to your taste preferences.

Ingredients:

- 1 cup all-purpose flour
- 2 large eggs
- 1 cup milk
- 1/4 cup water
- 1/4 tsp salt
- 1/4 cup vegetable oil
- 2 cups fresh baby spinach leaves, washed and dried
- 1/2 cup crumbled feta cheese
- 2 cloves garlic, minced
- 1 tbsp olive oil
- Salt and pepper to taste

Instructions:

1. In a mixing bowl, whisk together flour, eggs, milk, water, salt, and vegetable oil until the batter is smooth.
2. Cover the bowl and let the batter rest for at least 30 minutes at room temperature.
3. In a separate pan, heat olive oil over medium heat.
4. Add minced garlic and sauté for 1-2 minutes until fragrant.
5. Add fresh spinach leaves and sauté until wilted, about 2-3 minutes.
6. Remove the spinach from the heat and let it cool slightly.
7. In a mixing bowl, combine the cooked spinach, and crumbled feta cheese, and season with salt and pepper to taste.
8. Heat a non-stick skillet over medium heat.

9. Pour 1/4 cup of the crepe batter onto the skillet and swirl to evenly spread the batter.
10. Cook the crepe for about 1 minute on one side or until the edges turn golden brown.
11. Flip the crepe over and cook the other side for another 30 seconds.
12. Once all the crepes are cooked, add 1-2 tablespoons of the spinach and feta mixture on one-half of the crepe.
13. Fold the other half of the crepe over the filling and gently press down.
14. Place the crepe on a plate and sprinkle some extra feta cheese on top, if desired.
15. Repeat with the remaining crepes and filling.

Bacon, Egg & Cheese Brunch Crepes

If you're looking for a delicious and creative way to enjoy brunch, look no further than bacon, egg & cheese brunch crepes! This savory breakfast dish is easy to make and will impress your guests with its gourmet flavor. For an added twist, use your favorite type of cheese or mix and match different ones to create a unique flavor.

Ingredients:

- ✓ 1 cup all-purpose flour
- ✓ 2 large eggs
- ✓ 1 cup milk
- ✓ 1/4 cup water
- ✓ 1/4 tsp salt
- ✓ 1/4 cup vegetable oil
- ✓ 4 slices bacon, cooked and crumbled
- ✓ 4 large eggs
- ✓ 1/2 cup shredded cheddar cheese
- ✓ Salt and pepper to taste
- ✓ Tomato sauce and mayonnaise to taste

Instructions:

1. In a mixing bowl, whisk together flour, eggs, milk, water, salt, and vegetable oil until the batter is smooth.
2. Cover the bowl and let the batter rest for at least 30 minutes at room temperature.
3. Heat a non-stick skillet over medium heat and cook the bacon until crispy.
4. Remove the bacon from the skillet and let it cool. Once cooled, crumble the bacon into small pieces.
5. Heat a non-stick skillet over medium heat.
6. Pour 1/4 cup of the crepe batter onto the skillet and swirl to evenly spread the batter.
7. Cook the crepe for about 1 minute on one side or until the edges turn golden brown.

8. Flip the crepe over and cook the other side for another 30 seconds.
9. Once all the crepes are cooked, add 1-2 eggs to the crepe batter and swirl to evenly spread the eggs.
10. Add 1-2 tablespoons of crumbled bacon and shredded cheddar cheese to one-half of the crepe.
11. Topped with salt, pepper, tomato sauce, and mayonnaise.
12. Fold the other half of the crepe over the filling and gently press down.
13. Place the crepe on a plate and sprinkle some chopped fresh chives on top.
14. Repeat with the remaining crepes and filling.

Chicken salad Crepes

Chicken salad crepes are a delicious and versatile dish that can be enjoyed for breakfast, lunch, or dinner. This recipe will provide an overview of the history of chicken salad crepes and tips and techniques for preparing them to create your culinary masterpiece.

Ingredients:

- ✓ 1 cup all-purpose flour
- ✓ 2 large eggs
- ✓ 1 cup milk
- ✓ 1/4 cup water
- ✓ 1/4 tsp salt
- ✓ 1/4 cup vegetable oil
- ✓ 2 cups cooked chicken, diced or shredded
- ✓ 1/4 cup mayonnaise
- ✓ 1/4 cup diced red onion
- ✓ 1/4 cup diced apple
- ✓ 1/4 cup lettuce
- ✓ 1/4 cup tomatoes
- ✓ 1/4 cup cucumber
- ✓ 1/4 cup bell pepper
- ✓ Salt and pepper to taste

Instructions:

1. In a mixing bowl, whisk together flour, eggs, milk, water, salt, and vegetable oil until the batter is smooth.
2. Cover the bowl and let the batter rest for at least 30 minutes at room temperature.
3. In a separate bowl, mix cooked chicken, mayonnaise, lettuce, tomatoes, cucumber, bell pepper, diced red onion, and diced apple until well combined.
4. Heat a non-stick skillet over medium heat.
5. Pour 1/4 cup of the crepe batter onto the skillet and swirl to evenly spread the batter.

6. Cook the crepe for about 1 minute on one side or until the edges turn golden brown.
7. Flip the crepe over and cook the other side for another 30 seconds.
8. Once all the crepes are cooked, add 1-2 tablespoons of the chicken salad mixture on one-half of the crepe.
9. Fold the other half of the crepe over the filling and gently press down.
10. Place the crepe on a plate and sprinkle some chopped fresh parsley on top.
11. Repeat with the remaining crepes and filling.

Mushroom & Truffle Oil Delight Crepes

Crepes are a delightful treat that can be enjoyed as a savory or sweet dish. If you're looking for something with a luxurious twist on traditional crepes, the Mushroom & Truffle Oil Delight Crepes will not disappoint. The combination of mushrooms, truffle oil, and cheese creates an unforgettable flavor that will have you savoring every bite. This delicious recipe is easy to make and requires only a few common ingredients that can be found in most households.

Ingredients:

- 1 cup all-purpose flour
- 2 large eggs
- 1 cup milk
- 1/4 cup water
- 1/4 tsp salt
- 1/4 cup vegetable oil
- 2 cups sliced mushrooms
- 1 tbsp truffle oil
- 1/2 cup grated Parmesan cheese
- 2 tbsp chopped fresh parsley
- Salt and pepper to taste

Instructions:

1. In a mixing bowl, whisk together flour, eggs, milk, water, salt, and vegetable oil until the batter is smooth.
2. Cover the bowl and let the batter rest for at least 30 minutes at room temperature.
3. In a separate pan, heat truffle oil over medium heat.
4. Add sliced mushrooms and sauté for 4-5 minutes until tender and lightly browned.
5. Remove the mushrooms from the heat and let them cool slightly.
6. In a mixing bowl, combine the cooked mushrooms and grated Parmesan cheese, and season with salt and pepper to taste.
7. Heat a non-stick skillet over medium heat.

8. Pour 1/4 cup of the crepe batter onto the skillet and swirl to evenly spread the batter.
9. Cook the crepe for about 1 minute on one side or until the edges turn golden brown.
10. Flip the crepe over and cook the other side for another 30 seconds.
11. Once all the crepes are cooked, add 1-2 tablespoons of the mushroom and Parmesan mixture on one-half of the crepe.
12. Fold the other half of the crepe over the filling and gently press down.
13. Place the crepe on a plate and sprinkle some chopped fresh parsley on top.
14. Repeat with the remaining crepes and filling.

Ham, Egg & Cheese Breakfast Crepes

Breakfast is the most important meal of the day, so making something delicious and nutritious is essential. Ham, egg, and cheese breakfast crepes are a great way to start your day. These savory crepes combine your favorite breakfast ingredients into one yummy dish. Not only are they easy to make, but they are also simple enough for beginner cooks to make easily. Plus, they taste just as good as they look!

Ingredients:

- ✓ 1 cup all-purpose flour
- ✓ 2 large eggs
- ✓ 1 cup milk
- ✓ 1/4 cup water
- ✓ 1/4 tsp salt
- ✓ 1/4 cup vegetable oil
- ✓ 4 slices of ham, diced
- ✓ 4 large eggs
- ✓ 1/2 cup shredded cheddar cheese
- ✓ Salt and pepper to taste
- ✓ Tomato sauce and mayonnaise to taste

Instructions:

1. In a mixing bowl, whisk together flour, eggs, milk, water, salt, and vegetable oil until the batter is smooth.
2. Cover the bowl and let the batter rest for at least 30 minutes at room temperature.
3. Heat a non-stick skillet over medium heat.
4. Pour 1/4 cup of the crepe batter onto the skillet and swirl to evenly spread the batter.
5. Cook the crepe for about 1 minute on one side or until the edges start to turn golden brown.
6. Flip the crepe over and cook the other side for another 30 seconds.
7. Once all the crepes are cooked, add 1-2 eggs onto the crepe batter and swirl to evenly spread the eggs.

8. Add 1-2 tablespoons of the diced ham on one half of the crepe.
9. Sprinkle 1-2 tablespoons of the shredded cheddar cheese on top of the eggs and ham.
10. Topped with salt, pepper, tomato sauce, and mayonnaise.
11. Fold the other half of the crepe over the filling and gently press down.
12. Place the crepe on a plate and sprinkle some extra shredded cheddar cheese on top, if desired.
13. Repeat with the remaining crepes and filling.

Greek Chicken & Feta Savory Crepes

Are you looking for a delicious and easy meal to make? Then you should try these Greek Chicken & Feta Savory Crepes! They combine two classic flavors, feta cheese, and chicken, with a twist: they are served as crepes. This is an exciting way to liven up your dinner rotation with a dish that is both tasty and impressive. Not only are these crepes delicious, but they take minimal effort to prepare.

Ingredients:

- 1 cup all-purpose flour
- 2 large eggs
- 1 cup milk
- 1/4 cup water
- 1/4 tsp salt
- 1/4 cup vegetable oil
- 2 cups cooked chicken, diced
- 1/4 cup crumbled feta cheese
- 1/4 cup diced cucumber
- 1/4 cup diced tomato
- 1/4 cup diced red onion
- 2 tbsp chopped fresh parsley
- Salt and pepper to taste
- Tzatziki sauce (optional)

Instructions:

1. In a mixing bowl, whisk together flour, eggs, milk, water, salt, and vegetable oil until the batter is smooth.
2. Cover the bowl and let the batter rest for at least 30 minutes at room temperature.
3. In a separate bowl, mix cooked chicken, crumbled feta cheese, diced cucumber, diced tomato, diced red onion, and chopped parsley until well combined.
4. Season with salt and pepper to taste.
5. Heat a non-stick skillet over medium heat.

6. Pour 1/4 cup of the crepe batter onto the skillet and swirl to evenly spread the batter.
7. Cook the crepe for about 1 minute on one side or until the edges start to turn golden brown.
8. Flip the crepe over and cook the other side for another 30 seconds.
9. Once all the crepes are cooked, add 1-2 tablespoons of the chicken and feta mixture on one half of the crepe.
10. Drizzle some tzatziki sauce on top of the chicken and feta mixture, if desired.
11. Fold the other half of the crepe over the filling and gently press down.
12. Place the crepe on a plate and sprinkle some chopped fresh parsley on top.
13. Repeat with the remaining crepes and filling.

Smoked Salmon & Cream Cheese Brunch Crepes

If you're looking for an impressive brunch option, look no further than smoked salmon and cream cheese crepes. This dish is elegant, flavorful, and perfect for entertaining or a special Sunday breakfast. It's surprisingly simple to make, with only a few ingredients required, and the result is a beautiful presentation that everyone will love. Light, delicate crepes are filled with rich cream cheese and topped with luscious smoked salmon. A delicious blend of flavors creates an unforgettable dining experience.

Ingredients:

- 1 cup all-purpose flour
- 2 large eggs
- 1 cup milk
- 1/4 cup water
- 1/4 tsp salt
- 1/4 cup vegetable oil
- 4 oz. smoked salmon, sliced
- 4 oz. cream cheese, softened
- 2 tbsp chopped fresh dill
- Salt and pepper to taste

Instructions:

1. In a mixing bowl, whisk together flour, eggs, milk, water, salt, and vegetable oil until the batter is smooth.
2. Cover the bowl and let the batter rest for at least 30 minutes at room temperature.
3. In a separate bowl, mix softened cream cheese and chopped fresh dill until well combined.
4. Heat a non-stick skillet over medium heat.
5. Pour 1/4 cup of the crepe batter onto the skillet and swirl to evenly spread the batter.
6. Cook the crepe for about 1 minute on one side or until the edges start to turn golden brown.

7. Flip the crepe over and cook the other side for another 30 seconds.
8. Once all the crepes are cooked, spread 1-2 tablespoons of the cream cheese mixture onto one half of the crepe.
9. Add a few slices of smoked salmon on top of the cream cheese mixture.
10. Season with salt and pepper to taste.
11. Fold the other half of the crepe over the filling and gently press down.
12. Place the crepe on a plate and sprinkle some extra chopped fresh dill on top, if desired.
13. Repeat with the remaining crepes and filling.

Mixed Berry Rainbow Crepes

If you're looking for a fun and delicious way to brighten breakfast, look no further than mixed berry rainbow crepes! These beautiful and tasty crepes will surely put a smile on everyone's face. Packed with healthy berries, these colorful crepes are simple to make and bring a unique twist to your morning routine. They look amazing, and their sweet and fruity flavors make them the perfect way to start your day.

Ingredients:

- ✓ 1 cup all-purpose flour
- ✓ 2 large eggs
- ✓ 1 cup milk
- ✓ 1/4 cup water
- ✓ 1/4 tsp salt
- ✓ 1/4 cup vegetable oil
- ✓ Food coloring in multiple colors (red, orange, yellow, green, blue, purple)
- ✓ 2 cups mixed berries (such as strawberries, blueberries, raspberries, and blackberries)
- ✓ 1/4 cup powdered sugar
- ✓ 1/4 cup honey
- ✓ Whipped cream and sauce (optional)

Instructions:

1. In a mixing bowl, whisk together flour, eggs, milk, water, salt, and vegetable oil until the batter is smooth.
2. Divide the batter evenly into six separate bowls.
3. Add a few drops of food coloring to each bowl, stirring until the batter is fully colored.
4. Heat a non-stick skillet over medium heat.
5. Pour a small amount of the colored batter (about 1 tablespoon) of all 6 colored onto the skillet, spreading it out to form a thin circle.

Stack them in the order of the rainbow colors (red, orange, yellow, green, blue, purple).
6. Cook the crepe for about 30 seconds on one side or until the edges start to turn slightly golden.
7. Flip the crepe over and cook the other side for 10-15 seconds.

8. Once all the crepes are cooked, place 1-2 tablespoons of the mixed berry mixture onto one half of the crepe stack. And it is topped with honey.
9. Fold the other half of the crepe over the filling and gently press down.
10. Garnish the crepes with whipped cream, powdered sugar, and sauce, if desired.

Mango Sticky Rice Crepe

Mango sticky rice crepes are an indulgent way to satisfy your sweet tooth. A combination of heavenly ingredients, these crepes have a unique taste with sweetness, creaminess, and texture. Although often associated with traditional Thai cuisine, this delightful dessert can be enjoyed by everyone around the world.

Ingredients:

- ✓ 1 cup all-purpose flour
- ✓ 2 large eggs
- ✓ 1 cup milk
- ✓ 1/4 cup water
- ✓ 1/4 tsp salt
- ✓ 1/4 cup vegetable oil
- ✓ 1 cup sticky rice, cooked
- ✓ 1 cup coconut milk
- ✓ 1/4 cup sugar
- ✓ 1/4 tsp salt
- ✓ 1 ripe mango, peeled and diced
- ✓ 1/4 cup shredded coconut (optional)
- ✓ Whipped cream and mango sauce (optional)

Instructions:

1. In a mixing bowl, whisk together flour, eggs, milk, water, salt, and vegetable oil until the batter is smooth.
2. Cover the bowl and let the batter rest for at least 30 minutes at room temperature.
3. In a separate pan, combine cooked sticky rice, coconut milk, sugar, and salt over medium heat.
4. Cook for 10-12 minutes, occasionally stirring until the mixture thickens and the rice is tender.
5. Remove the pan from heat and let the mixture cool slightly.
6. Heat a non-stick skillet over medium heat.

7. Pour 1/4 cup of the crepe batter onto the skillet and swirl to evenly spread the batter.
8. Cook the crepe for about 1 minute on one side or until the edges start to turn golden brown.
9. Flip the crepe over and cook the other side for another 30 seconds.
10. Once all the crepes are cooked, add 1-2 tablespoons of the sticky rice mixture on one half of the crepe.
11. Add some diced mango on top of the sticky rice.
12. Fold the other half of the crepe over the filling and gently press down.
13. Sprinkle some toasted shredded coconut, Whipped cream, and mango sauce on top of the crepe, if desired.
14. Repeat with the remaining crepes and filling.

Blueberry Bliss Crepes

Do you love the sweet and tart taste of blueberries? Have you been searching for a new way to incorporate this delicious fruit into your diet? Look no further - these blueberry bliss crepes will surely become a new favorite in your home. With just a few simple ingredients, this delectable breakfast or snack will tantalize your taste buds and have everyone begging for more.

Ingredients:

- 1 cup all-purpose flour
- 2 large eggs
- 1 cup milk
- 1/4 cup water
- 1/4 tsp salt
- 1/4 cup vegetable oil
- 2 cups fresh blueberries
- 1/4 cup sugar
- 2 tbsp cornstarch
- 1/4 cup water
- Whipped cream (optional)

Instructions:

1. In a mixing bowl, whisk together flour, eggs, milk, water, salt, and vegetable oil until the batter is smooth.
2. Cover the bowl and let the batter rest for at least 30 minutes at room temperature.
3. In a separate pan, combine fresh blueberries and sugar over medium heat.
4. Cook for 5-7 minutes, occasionally stirring until the blueberries start to break down and release their juices.
5. In a small bowl, whisk together cornstarch and water until well combined.
6. Add the cornstarch mixture to the blueberry mixture and cook for an additional 1-2 minutes until the mixture thickens.

7. Remove the pan from heat and let the mixture cool slightly.
8. Heat a non-stick skillet over medium heat.
9. Pour 1/4 cup of the crepe batter onto the skillet and swirl to evenly spread the batter.
10. Cook the crepe for about 1 minute on one side or until the edges start to turn golden brown.
11. Flip the crepe over and cook the other side for another 30 seconds.
12. Once all the crepes are cooked, add 1-2 tablespoons of the blueberry mixture on one half of the crepe.
13. Fold the other half of the crepe over the filling and gently press down.
14. Repeat with the remaining crepes and filling.
15. Garnish the crepes with a dollop of whipped cream, if desired.

Caramelized Apple Spice Crepes

Fall is the perfect time to indulge in delicious treats, and one of the best fall desserts to make is caramelized apple spice crepes. This recipe can be made in under an hour and is a great way to use seasonal ingredients like apples and pumpkin spice. So whether you're making a casual brunch for friends or an impressive dessert for family, these crepes are sure to please everyone.

Ingredients:

- 1 cup all-purpose flour
- 2 large eggs
- 1 cup milk
- 1/4 cup water
- 1/4 tsp salt
- 1/4 cup vegetable oil
- 2 tbsp butter
- 2 apples, peeled and sliced
- 1/4 cup brown sugar
- 1 tsp cinnamon
- 1/4 tsp nutmeg
- Whipped cream (optional)

Instructions:

1. In a mixing bowl, whisk together flour, eggs, milk, water, salt, and vegetable oil until the batter is smooth.
2. Cover the bowl and let the batter rest for at least 30 minutes at room temperature.
3. In a separate pan, melt butter over medium heat.
4. Add sliced apples to the pan and cook for 5-7 minutes until the apples start to soften.
5. Add brown sugar, cinnamon, and nutmeg to the pan, stirring to coat the apples.
6. Cook for an additional 5-7 minutes until the apples are caramelized and tender.

7. Remove the pan from heat and let the mixture cool slightly.
8. Heat a non-stick skillet over medium heat.
9. Pour 1/4 cup of the crepe batter onto the skillet and swirl to evenly spread the batter.
10. Cook the crepe for about 1 minute on one side or until the edges start to turn golden brown.
11. Flip the crepe over and cook the other side for another 30 seconds.
12. Once all the crepes are cooked, add 1-2 tablespoons of the caramelized apple mixture on one half of the crepe.
13. Fold the other half of the crepe over the filling and gently press down.
14. Repeat with the remaining crepes and filling.
15. Garnish the crepes with a dollop of whipped cream, if desired.

Chocolate Hazelnut Cream Crepes

If you're looking for an indulgent breakfast or brunch treat, look no further than chocolate hazelnut cream crepes. This easy-to-make recipe combines two classic flavors - dark chocolate and hazelnut - with a light and airy crepe base. These crepes will satisfy your sweet tooth, but they are surprisingly simple to make and require just a few ingredients you likely already have in your pantry.

Ingredients:

- ✓ 1 cup all-purpose flour
- ✓ 2 large eggs
- ✓ 1 cup milk
- ✓ 1/4 cup water
- ✓ 1/4 tsp salt
- ✓ 1/4 cup vegetable oil
- ✓ 1/2 cup chocolate hazelnut spread (such as Nutella)
- ✓ 1/4 cup chopped hazelnuts
- ✓ 1/4 cup chopped almonds
- ✓ Whipped cream and chocolate sauce (optional)

Instructions:

1. In a mixing bowl, whisk together flour, eggs, milk, water, salt, and vegetable oil until the batter is smooth.
2. Cover the bowl and let the batter rest for at least 30 minutes at room temperature.
3. Heat a non-stick skillet over medium heat.
4. Pour 1/4 cup of the crepe batter onto the skillet and swirl to evenly spread the batter.
5. Cook the crepe for about 1 minute on one side or until the edges start to turn golden brown.
6. Flip the crepe over and cook the other side for another 30 seconds.
7. Once all the crepes are cooked, spread 1-2 tablespoons of chocolate hazelnut spread onto one half of the crepe.

8. Sprinkle some chopped hazelnuts and almonds on top of the chocolate hazelnut spread.
9. Fold the other half of the crepe over the filling and gently press down.
10. Repeat with the remaining crepes and filling.
11. Garnish the crepes with whipped cream and chocolate sauce, if desired.

Honey and Raspberry Delight Crepes

Are you looking for a delicious breakfast that is also easy to make? Then, honey and Raspberry Delight Crepes might be the perfect recipe for you! This sweet, fruity treat will surely please even the pickiest of eaters. With simple ingredients like crepes, honey, raspberries, and cream cheese, this dish requires minimal preparation and cooking time. Best of all, it's a delicious way to start your morning off right!

Ingredients:

- ✓ 1 cup all-purpose flour
- ✓ 2 large eggs
- ✓ 1 cup milk
- ✓ 1/4 cup water
- ✓ 1/4 tsp salt
- ✓ 1/4 cup vegetable oil
- ✓ 1/4 cup honey
- ✓ 1 cup fresh raspberries
- ✓ Whipped cream (optional)

Instructions:

1. In a mixing bowl, whisk together flour, eggs, milk, water, salt, and vegetable oil until the batter is smooth.
2. Cover the bowl and let the batter rest for at least 30 minutes at room temperature.
3. Heat a non-stick skillet over medium heat.
4. Pour 1/4 cup of the crepe batter onto the skillet and swirl to evenly spread the batter.
5. Cook the crepe for about 1 minute on one side or until the edges start to turn golden brown.
6. Flip the crepe over and cook the other side for another 30 seconds.
7. Once all the crepes are cooked, drizzle 1-2 tablespoons of honey onto one half of the crepe.
8. Add a few fresh raspberries on top of the honey.

9. Fold the other half of the crepe over the filling and gently press down.
10. Repeat with the remaining crepes and filling.
11. Garnish the crepes with a dollop of whipped cream, if desired.

Sweet Potato Cinnamon Roll Crepes

If you're looking for a delicious and unique way to start your morning, why not try Sweet Potato Cinnamon Roll Crepes? These mouth-watering crepes make the perfect breakfast treat, combining the classic flavors of cinnamon rolls with the sweetness of the sweet potato. Not only are they easy to make at home, but they also look great when served! Made with simple ingredients like flour, butter, and spices, these crepes satisfy anyone's cravings for something sweet.

Ingredients:

- ✓ 1 cup all-purpose flour
- ✓ 2 large eggs
- ✓ 1 cup milk
- ✓ 1/4 cup water
- ✓ 1/4 tsp salt
- ✓ 1/4 cup vegetable oil
- ✓ 1 large sweet potato, peeled and cubed
- ✓ 1/4 cup brown sugar
- ✓ 1 tsp cinnamon
- ✓ 1/4 tsp nutmeg
- ✓ 1/4 cup cream cheese, softened
- ✓ 1/4 cup powdered sugar
- ✓ Whipped cream (optional)

Instructions:

1. In a mixing bowl, whisk together flour, eggs, milk, water, salt, and vegetable oil until the batter is smooth.
2. Cover the bowl and let the batter rest for at least 30 minutes at room temperature.
3. In a separate pan, boil the cubed sweet potato until tender.
4. Drain the sweet potato and return it to the pan.
5. Add brown sugar, cinnamon, and nutmeg to the pan, stirring to coat the sweet potato.

6. Mash the sweet potato mixture until it is smooth and well combined.
7. In a separate bowl, mix softened cream cheese and powdered sugar until well combined.
8. Heat a non-stick skillet over medium heat.
9. Pour 1/4 cup of the crepe batter onto the skillet and swirl to evenly spread the batter.
10. Cook the crepe for about 1 minute on one side or until the edges start to turn golden brown.
11. Flip the crepe over and cook the other side for another 30 seconds.
12. Once all the crepes are cooked, spread 1-2 tablespoons of the sweet potato mixture onto one half of the crepe.
13. Add a dollop of the cream cheese mixture on top of the sweet potato mixture.
14. Roll the crepe up like a cinnamon roll and slice it into rounds.
15. Repeat with the remaining crepes and filling.
16. Garnish the crepes with a dollop of whipped cream, if desired.

Tiramisu Lover's Crepes

If you love tiramisu flavors but are looking for something a bit heartier, look no further than Tiramisu Lover's Crepes! This delicious twist on a classic French dessert combines tiramisu's sweet and creamy flavors with the satisfying crunch of crepes. These delightful treats are perfect for brunch, after-dinner desserts, or indulgent snacks.

Ingredients:

- 1 cup all-purpose flour
- 2 large eggs
- 1 cup milk
- 1/4 cup water
- 1/4 tsp salt
- 1/4 cup vegetable oil
- 1/2 cup mascarpone cheese
- 1/4 cup powdered sugar
- 1/4 cup heavy cream
- 2 tbsp coffee liqueur or strong brewed coffee
- 1/4 cup cocoa powder
- Whipped cream and chocolate shavings (optional)

Instructions:

1. In a mixing bowl, whisk together flour, eggs, milk, water, salt, and vegetable oil until the batter is smooth.
2. Cover the bowl and let the batter rest for at least 30 minutes at room temperature.
3. In a separate bowl, mix mascarpone cheese and powdered sugar until well combined.
4. In a separate bowl, whip the heavy cream until it forms stiff peaks.
5. Fold the whipped cream into the mascarpone mixture until well combined.
6. Stir in the coffee liqueur or strong brewed coffee.
7. Heat a non-stick skillet over medium heat.

8. Pour 1/4 cup of the crepe batter onto the skillet and swirl to evenly spread the batter.
9. Cook the crepe for about 1 minute on one side or until the edges start to turn golden brown.
10. Flip the crepe over and cook the other side for another 30 seconds.
11. Once all the crepes are cooked, add 1-2 tablespoons of the mascarpone mixture on one half of the crepe.
12. Sprinkle some cocoa powder on top of the mascarpone mixture.
13. Fold the other half of the crepe over the filling and gently press down.
14. Repeat with the remaining crepes and filling.
15. Garnish the crepes with whipped cream and some chocolate shavings, if desired.

Matcha Green Tea Delight Crepes

Matcha Green Tea Delight Crepes are a delicious and unique way to enjoy this popular green tea in a delectable crepe. These tempting treats make for a perfect afternoon snack or light breakfast. They can also be an after-dinner dessert that won't leave you feeling overly full. You can quickly create this delightful dish with the right ingredients and a few simple steps.

Ingredients:

- 1 cup all-purpose flour
- 2 large eggs
- 1 cup milk
- 1/4 cup water
- 1/4 tsp salt
- 1/4 cup vegetable oil
- 2 tsp matcha green tea powder
- 1/4 cup granulated sugar
- Whipped cream
- Ice cream and fresh fruit (optional)

Instructions:

1. In a mixing bowl, whisk together flour, eggs, milk, water, salt, vegetable oil, and 1 tsp matcha green tea powder until the batter is smooth.
2. Cover the bowl and let the batter rest for at least 30 minutes at room temperature.
3. Heat a non-stick skillet over medium heat.
4. Pour 1/4 cup of the crepe batter onto the skillet and swirl to evenly spread the batter.
5. Cook the crepe for about 1 minute on one side or until the edges start to turn golden brown.
6. Flip the crepe over and cook the other side for another 30 seconds.
7. Once all the crepes are cooked, add whipped cream and matcha green tea on one half of the crepe.

8. Fold the crepe into quarters or roll it up. Sprinkle the matcha green tea mixture on top of the crepe.
9. Repeat with the remaining crepes and filling.
10. Serve the crepes with a dollop of whipped cream, some fresh fruit, and ice cream, if desired.

Tropical Island Paradise Crepes

Welcome to a paradise of sweet and savory flavors! If you're looking for something unique and delicious, tropical island paradise crepes will surely hit the spot. These treats are made with a thin, fluffy crepe batter filled with your favorite ingredients like pineapple, mango, coconut, and more. With just the right balance of sweetness and texture, these delightful crepes make a great breakfast, lunch, or dinner option.

Ingredients:

- 1 cup all-purpose flour
- 2 large eggs
- 1 cup milk
- 1/4 cup water
- 1/4 tsp salt
- 1/4 cup vegetable oil
- 1 cup fresh pineapple, chopped
- 1 cup fresh mango, chopped
- 1/2 cup sweetened coconut flakes
- 1/4 cup honey
- Whipped cream (optional)
- Ice cream (optional)

Instructions:

1. In a mixing bowl, whisk together flour, eggs, milk, water, salt, and vegetable oil until the batter is smooth.
2. Cover the bowl and let the batter rest for at least 30 minutes at room temperature.
3. In a separate pan, heat the chopped pineapple and mango over medium heat until they start to soften.
4. Add sweetened coconut flakes to the pan and stir to combine.
5. Cook for 1-2 minutes until the mixture is heated through.
6. Remove the pan from heat and let the mixture cool slightly.
7. Heat a non-stick skillet over medium heat.

8. Pour 1/4 cup of the crepe batter onto the skillet and swirl to evenly spread the batter.
9. Cook the crepe for about 1 minute on one side or until the edges start to turn golden brown.
10. Flip the crepe over and cook the other side for another 30 seconds.
11. Once all the crepes are cooked, add 1-2 tablespoons of the tropical fruit mixture on one half of the crepe.
12. Drizzle some honey on top of the fruit mixture.
13. Fold the other half of the crepe over the filling and gently press down.
14. Repeat with the remaining crepes and filling.
15. Garnish the crepes with a dollop of whipped cream and Ice cream, if desired.

Fruit Lovers' Crepes

Do you love fruit? Do you have a sweet tooth for something light and airy? If so, then this recipe is perfect for you! Fruit Lovers' Crepes are a delicious way to satisfy your craving. Not only are they easy to make, but they are also highly customizable based on what type of fruit you prefer. So whether it's strawberries, bananas, or blueberries, crepes can be tailored to suit any occasion.

Ingredients:

- 1 cup all-purpose flour
- 2 large eggs
- 1 cup milk
- 1/4 cup water
- 1/4 tsp salt
- 1/4 cup vegetable oil
- 2 cups mixed fresh fruits (such as strawberries, kiwis, and melons)
- Strawberry sauce
- Whipped cream (optional)
- Ice cream (optional)

Instructions:

1. In a mixing bowl, whisk together flour, eggs, milk, water, salt, and vegetable oil until the batter is smooth.
2. Cover the bowl and let the batter rest for at least 30 minutes at room temperature.
3. Heat a non-stick skillet over medium heat.
4. Pour 1/4 cup of the crepe batter onto the skillet and swirl to evenly spread the batter.
5. Cook the crepe for about 1 minute on one side or until the edges start to turn golden brown.
6. Flip the crepe over and cook the other side for another 30 seconds.
7. Once all the crepes are cooked, add whipped cream and a few spoonfuls of the mixed fruit on top of the whipped cream on one half of the crepe.

8. Topped with strawberry sauce.
9. Fold the other half of the crepe over the filling and gently press down.
10. Repeat with the remaining crepes and filling.
11. Garnish the crepes with a dollop of whipped cream and Ice cream, if desired.

Mochi Brownie Chocolate Crepes

If you're looking for a new, delicious dessert to make with your family or friends, look no further than Mochi Brownie Chocolate Crepes! This indulgent treat is sure to satisfy any sweet tooth. The crepes are made with a simple crepe batter and can be filled with mochi, brownies, and chocolate chips for a double layer of sweetness.

Ingredients:

- 1 cup all-purpose flour
- 2 large eggs
- 1 cup milk
- 1/4 cup water
- 1/4 tsp salt
- 1/4 cup vegetable oil
- 1/4 cup unsweetened cocoa powder
- 1/4 cup powdered sugar
- 1/4 cup honey
- Mochi pieces
- Brownie pieces
- Whipped cream (optional)
- Ice cream (optional)

Instructions:

1. In a mixing bowl, whisk together flour, eggs, milk, water, salt, vegetable oil, unsweetened cocoa powder, and granulated sugar until the batter is smooth.
2. Cover the bowl and let the batter rest for at least 30 minutes at room temperature.
3. Heat a non-stick skillet over medium heat.
4. Pour 1/4 cup of the crepe batter onto the skillet and swirl to evenly spread the batter.
5. Cook the crepe for about 1 minute on one side or until the edges start to turn golden brown.
6. Flip the crepe over and cook the other side for another 30 seconds.

7. Once all the crepes are cooked, add a few pieces of mochi and brownie on one half of the crepe.
8. Drizzle some honey on top of the mochi and brownie.
9. Fold the other half of the crepe over the filling and gently press down.
10. Repeat with the remaining crepes and filling.
11. Garnish the crepes with whipped cream, powdered sugar, and Ice cream, if desired.

Nutella Banana Cereal Crepes

Nothing beats a delicious and indulgent breakfast, especially on the weekends. So if you're looking for something new to try in the kitchen, why not whip up these decadent Nutella Banana Cereal Crepes? These crepes are filled with a creamy Nutella spread and crunchy cereal pieces, finished with sweet sliced banana. Not only are they scrumptious, but they come together quickly and easily.

Ingredients:

- ✓ 1 cup all-purpose flour
- ✓ 2 large eggs
- ✓ 1 cup milk
- ✓ 1/4 cup water
- ✓ 1/4 tsp salt
- ✓ 1/4 cup vegetable oil
- ✓ 1/4 cup Nutella spread
- ✓ 2 bananas, sliced
- ✓ 1/2 cup cereal of your choice (such as granola, cornflakes, or rice crisps)
- ✓ Chocolate sauce
- ✓ Whipped cream (optional)
- ✓ Ice cream (optional)

Instructions:

1. In a mixing bowl, whisk together flour, eggs, milk, water, salt, and vegetable oil until the batter is smooth.
2. Cover the bowl and let the batter rest for at least 30 minutes at room temperature.
3. Heat a non-stick skillet over medium heat.
4. Pour 1/4 cup of the crepe batter onto the skillet and swirl to evenly spread the batter.
5. Cook the crepe for about 1 minute on one side or until the edges start to turn golden brown.
6. Flip the crepe over and cook the other side for another 30 seconds.

7. Once all the crepes are cooked, add 1-2 tablespoons of Nutella spread on one half of the crepe.
8. Add a few slices of banana and cereal on top of the Nutella. And topped with chocolate sauce.
9. Fold the other half of the crepe over the filling and gently press down.
10. Repeat with the remaining crepes and filling.
11. Garnish the crepes with a dollop of whipped cream and Ice cream, if desired.

Apple Pie Cinnamon Roll Crepes

Apple Pie Cinnamon Roll Crepes are a delicious and creative combination of two classic desserts. These tasty treats will surely be a favorite among kids and adults alike. This recipe is easy to make with simple ingredients that you can find at most grocery stores. Combining the flavors of an apple pie and a cinnamon roll, these crepes have just the right sweetness to satisfy any sweet tooth. The result is a delicious dessert that will make your kitchen smell amazing!

Ingredients:

- 1 cup all-purpose flour
- 2 large eggs
- 1 cup milk
- 1/4 cup water
- 1/4 tsp salt
- 1/4 cup vegetable oil
- 2 cups apples, peeled and diced
- 1/4 cup granulated sugar
- 1 tsp ground cinnamon
- 1/4 tsp ground nutmeg
- 1/4 cup butter, melted
- 1/4 cup brown sugar
- 1/4 cup raisins (optional)
- Whipped cream (optional)

Instructions:

1. In a mixing bowl, whisk together flour, eggs, milk, water, salt, and vegetable oil until the batter is smooth.
2. Cover the bowl and let the batter rest for at least 30 minutes at room temperature.
3. In a separate pan, heat apples over medium heat until they start to soften.
4. Add granulated sugar, ground cinnamon, and ground nutmeg to the pan and stir to combine.

5. Cook for an additional 1-2 minutes until the mixture is heated through and the sugar is dissolved.
6. In a separate bowl, mix together melted butter and brown sugar until well combined.
7. Add raisins (optional) to the butter mixture and stir to combine.
8. Heat a non-stick skillet over medium heat.
9. Pour 1/4 cup of the crepe batter onto the skillet and swirl to evenly spread the batter.
10. Cook the crepe for about 1 minute on one side or until the edges start to turn golden brown.
11. Flip the crepe over and cook the other side for another 30 seconds.
12. Once all the crepes are cooked, add a spoonful of the apple pie mixture on one half of the crepe.
13. Add a spoonful of the butter mixture on top of the apple pie mixture.
14. Fold the other half of the crepe over the filling and gently press down.
15. Repeat with the remaining crepes and filling.
16. Garnish the crepes with a dollop of whipped cream, if desired.

Strawberry Shortcake Delight Crepes

If you're looking for a delicious breakfast recipe to tantalize your taste buds and make your kitchen smell like a bakery, try this delightful Strawberry Shortcake Delight Crepes recipe. Make these crepes and share them with friends or family for a special morning treat bursting with flavor! These crepes are perfect for any occasion – breakfast, brunch, or dessert – and have just the right sweetness.

Ingredients:

- 1 cup all-purpose flour
- 2 large eggs
- 1 cup milk
- 1/4 cup water
- 1/4 tsp salt
- 1/4 cup vegetable oil
- 2 cups fresh strawberries, sliced
- 1/4 cup granulated sugar
- 1/4 cup water
- 1 tbsp cornstarch
- 1 cup heavy cream
- 2 tbsp powdered sugar
- 1 tsp vanilla extract
- Whipped cream (optional)
- Ice cream (optional)

Instructions:

1. In a mixing bowl, whisk together flour, eggs, milk, water, salt, and vegetable oil until the batter is smooth.
2. Cover the bowl and let the batter rest for at least 30 minutes at room temperature.
3. In a separate pan, heat sliced strawberries over medium heat until they release their juices.
4. Add granulated sugar to the pan and stir to combine.

5. Cook for an additional 1-2 minutes until the mixture is heated through and the sugar is dissolved.
6. In a separate bowl, whisk together 1/4 cup water and cornstarch until well combined.
7. Add the cornstarch mixture to the strawberry mixture and stir until the sauce has thickened.
8. In another bowl, beat the heavy cream until soft peaks form.
9. Add powdered sugar and vanilla extract to the bowl and beat until stiff peaks form.
10. Heat a non-stick skillet over medium heat.
11. Pour 1/4 cup of the crepe batter onto the skillet and swirl to evenly spread the batter.
12. Cook the crepe for about 1 minute on one side or until the edges start to turn golden brown.
13. Flip the crepe over and cook the other side for another 30 seconds.
14. Once all the crepes are cooked, add a spoonful of the strawberry sauce on one half of the crepe.
15. Add a spoonful of whipped cream on top of the strawberry sauce.
16. Fold the other half of the crepe over the filling and gently press down.
17. Repeat with the remaining crepes and filling.
18. Garnish the crepes with whipped cream, Ice cream, and fresh strawberries, if desired.

Classic French Crepes Suzette (French Crepes with Orange)

Crepes Suzette is a classic French dessert that has existed for over a century. This simple yet exquisite dish consists of thin pancakes bathed in a luscious orange-flavored buttery sauce, making it the perfect treat for any occasion. The combination of sweet and savory flavors makes this dish sure to please even the pickiest palate.

Ingredients:

- 1 cup all-purpose flour
- 2 large eggs
- 1 cup milk
- 1/4 cup water
- 1/4 tsp salt
- 1/4 cup vegetable oil
- 2 oranges, juiced and zested
- 1/4 cup granulated sugar
- 1/4 cup water
- 2 tbsp unsalted butter
- Powdered sugar (optional)

Instructions:

1. In a mixing bowl, whisk together flour, eggs, milk, water, salt, and vegetable oil until the batter is smooth.
2. Cover the bowl and let the batter rest for at least 30 minutes at room temperature.
3. In a separate pan, heat orange juice and zest over medium heat until it starts to simmer.
4. Add granulated sugar to the pan and stir to combine.
5. Cook for an additional 1-2 minutes until the mixture is heated through and the sugar is dissolved.
6. In a separate pan, melt unsalted butter over medium heat.
7. Add 1/4 cup water to the butter and stir to combine.

8. Dip each crepe into the butter mixture, making sure both sides are coated.
9. Fold each crepe in half, and then fold in half again to form a triangle.
10. Add the crepes to the pan with the orange juice mixture and cook for 1-2 minutes on each side until the crepes are heated and the orange juice has been absorbed.
11. Remove the crepes from the pan and place them on a serving plate.
12. Dust the crepes with powdered sugar, if desired.
13. Garnish the crepes with fresh orange, if desired.

Honeyed Ricotta, Pistachio Delight And Almond Crepes

Do you have a sweet tooth and are looking for something special to tantalize your taste buds? Look no further! Our delicious recipe for Honeyed Ricotta, Pistachio Delight and Almond Crepes will satisfy your craving. This flavorful combination of savory ricotta cheese, crunchy pistachios and creamy almond crepes is the perfect way to end a meal or enjoy for dessert.

Ingredients:

- 1 cup all-purpose flour
- 2 large eggs
- 1 cup milk
- 1/4 cup water
- 1/4 tsp salt
- 1/4 cup vegetable oil
- 1 cup ricotta cheese
- 2 tbsp honey
- 1/4 cup shelled pistachios, chopped
- 1/4 cup slivered almonds
- Powdered sugar (optional)

Instructions:

1. In a mixing bowl, whisk together flour, eggs, milk, water, salt, and vegetable oil until the batter is smooth.
2. Cover the bowl and let the batter rest for at least 30 minutes at room temperature.
3. In a separate bowl, mix together ricotta cheese and honey until well combined.
4. Heat a non-stick skillet over medium heat.
5. Pour 1/4 cup of the crepe batter onto the skillet and swirl to evenly spread the batter.
6. Cook the crepe for about 1 minute on one side or until the edges start to turn golden brown.

7. Flip the crepe over and cook the other side for another 30 seconds.
8. Once all the crepes are cooked, spread a spoonful of the honeyed ricotta mixture on one half of the crepe.
9. Sprinkle chopped pistachios and slivered almonds on top of the ricotta mixture.
10. Fold the other half of the crepe over the filling and gently press down.
11. Repeat with the remaining crepes and filling.
12. Garnish the crepes with powdered sugar, if desired.

Peanut Butter Lovers' Crepes

Are you a fan of the classic combination of peanut butter and jelly? If so, then you're in luck; this recipe is all about celebrating the delectable duo with a delicious treat: peanut butter lovers' crepes! Whether you're looking for a quick snack or an impressive breakfast dish, these crepes will satisfy your craving. Not only are they easy to make, but they also provide an indulgent way to enjoy a favorite childhood flavor.

Ingredients:

- 1 cup all-purpose flour
- 2 large eggs
- 1 cup milk
- 1/4 cup water
- 1/4 tsp salt
- 1/4 cup vegetable oil
- 1/4 cup creamy peanut butter
- 2 ripe bananas, sliced
- 1 tbsp honey (optional)

Instructions:

1. In a mixing bowl, whisk together flour, eggs, milk, water, salt, and vegetable oil until the batter is smooth.
2. Cover the bowl and let the batter rest for at least 30 minutes at room temperature.
3. Heat a non-stick skillet over medium heat.
4. Pour 1/4 cup of the crepe batter onto the skillet and swirl to evenly spread the batter.
5. Cook the crepe for about 1 minute on one side or until the edges start to turn golden brown.
6. Flip the crepe over and cook the other side for another 30 seconds.
7. Once all the crepes are cooked, spread a spoonful of peanut butter on one half of the crepe.
8. Add a few slices of banana on top of the peanut butter.
9. Drizzle honey (optional) over the banana.

10. Fold the other half of the crepe over the filling and gently press down.
11. Repeat with the remaining crepes and filling.

Green Tea Crepe With Red Beans

Green tea crepe with red beans is an exquisite culinary delight that will tantalize your taste buds. This unique and delicious recipe pairs green tea crepes with sweet red bean paste, resulting in a delightful medley of savory and sweet flavors. With just five simple ingredients, you can whip up this delectable treat in no time.

Ingredients:

- 1 cup all-purpose flour
- 2 large eggs
- 1 cup milk
- 1/4 cup water
- 1/4 tsp salt
- 1/4 cup vegetable oil
- 2 tsp matcha green tea powder
- 1/4 cup granulated sugar
- 1/2 cup red beans, cooked and sweetened
- Whipped cream
- powdered sugar (optional)
- Ice cream (optional)

Instructions:

1. In a mixing bowl, whisk together flour, eggs, milk, water, salt, vegetable oil, and 1 tsp matcha green tea powder until the batter is smooth.
2. Cover the bowl and let the batter rest for at least 30 minutes at room temperature.
3. In a separate pan, heat red beans over medium heat until they are warmed through.
4. Add granulated sugar to the pan and stir to combine.
5. Cook for an additional 1-2 minutes until the mixture is heated through and the sugar is dissolved.
6. Heat a non-stick skillet over medium heat.

7. Pour 1/4 cup of the crepe batter onto the skillet and swirl to evenly spread the batter.
8. Cook the crepe for about 1 minute on one side or until the edges start to turn golden brown.
9. Flip the crepe over and cook the other side for another 30 seconds.
10. Once all the crepes are cooked, add whipped cream and a spoonful of the sweetened red bean mixture on one half of the crepe.
11. Fold the other half of the crepe over the filling and gently press down.
12. Repeat with the remaining crepes and filling.
13. Garnish the crepes with powdered sugar, Whipped cream and Ice cream, if desired.

NOTE:

NOTE: